TREETOPS

TI
CHRON

The Will of the People

Written by David Hunt
and illustrated by Alex Brychta

OXFORD
UNIVERSITY PRESS

OXFORD
UNIVERSITY PRESS

Great Clarendon Street, Oxford OX2 6DP, United Kingdom

Oxford University Press is a department of the University of Oxford.
It furthers the University's objective of excellence in research, scholarship,
and education by publishing worldwide. Oxford is a registered trade mark of Oxford University Press
in the UK and in certain other countries

Text written by David Hunt, based on the original characters created
by Roderick Hunt and Alex Brychta

First Edition published in 2012

British Library Cataloguing in Publication Data

Data available

ISBN: 978-0-19-8475682

10 9 8 7 6 5 4 3

Printed in China by Imago

Paper used in the production of this book is a natural, recyclable product
made from wood grown in sustainable forests. The manufacturing process
conforms to the environmental regulations of the country of origin.

Acknowledgements: The publisher and authors would like to thank the following for their permission to reproduce photographs and other copyright material:

P46 Valentin Agapov/Shutterstock; Picsfive/Shutterstock; Hoberman Collection/Corbis; Valeriy Aksak/Shutterstock; PoodlesRock/Corbis; Jon Arnold/JAI/Corbis; Bettmann/Corbis; **PP 46-47** Techlogica/ Shutterstock; Jakub Krechowicz/Shutterstock; Blaz Kure/Shutterstock; **P47** Christie's Images/Corbis; Eric Gevaert/Shutterstock; National Geographic Society/Corbis; Ragnarock/Shutterstock

Chapter 1

The potter had waited at the harbour all morning for the trade boats to come. Beside him, on the busy quayside, were crates of his pots, jugs and bowls. They were to be carried across the sea to the scattered Greek islands. Then the boats would return to the mainland laden with goods to be sold in the great city of Athens. Boats carrying oil, or leather, or grain, others with cargos of silver, honey, wine or marble sailed back and forth over the bright sea.

Within the straw-packed crates, glimpses of the pots could be seen. Each one was beautifully decorated with images of Greek gods, mythical heroes and strange beasts

These images came from famous stories that everyone knew and loved. But not all the images were of myths and legends. Scenes from history were also glazed into some of the pots – in particular, Athens' long struggle against the Persians.

The Persians had invaded and ruled Athens for many years, before finally being driven out – but not before the Persian army had left its mark. Athens had been smashed. Even now, many years later, ruined parts of the city were still being rebuilt. But rebuilding was slow, and cost a great deal of money.

Recently, a long wall had been built around Athens. The section around the harbour was nearly finished. The potter watched the slaves lowering blocks of stone into place.

A woman stopped and spoke to the potter. "Walls around Athens are all very well," she sniffed. "But what about the people on the islands? They don't have walls around them. What protects *them* from invaders?"

The potter grunted, but did not reply.

At last, one by one, the boats returned. While the crates of pots were being lowered on to one of them, a cry went out across the harbour. "The Athenian councillors!" The potter turned to see a group of statesmen walking down towards the quay. The last crate of pottery was left dangling as the men stopped work and watched.

One of the councillors, Pericles, looked at the boatmen who stood bobbing up and down in their boats. "You have each been to one of the islands and delivered our message, I trust. Are the islanders coming to discuss the idea with the people of Athens?"

For a time no one dared to speak. All that could be heard was the sound of lapping water.

At last, one of the boatmen spoke. "O worthy councillors. As a protest, the islanders are not coming. They're outraged that you should even suggest ..."

One of the councillors twitched with anger. "They should have come! Our idea needs to be debated by the people ..."

Then, suddenly, the hoist that had been holding the crate gave way. The crate and its pots smashed to the ground.

“It’s a sign!” cried the councillor. “An omen! You see, Pericles! The gods are angry at your idea.”

Pericles smiled. “Perhaps. But those pots were for the islanders. If the gods are angry, it is with them, not us.”

Chapter 2

In the Time Vault, Mortlock was finishing a history lesson.

Kipper frowned. “Bad things that happen in history … surely the Virans can’t be behind all of them?”

Mortlock shook his head sadly. “No. Mankind is quite capable of doing such things too. That is why Virans are so hard to detect. They exploit history to attack anything positive mankind has created. Science, language, medicine, art, democracy …”

“Democracy?” asked Kipper.

“You know,” said Biff. “When everybody gets a say in how things are run. Votes and stuff.”

Kipper grinned. “No such thing when you’ve got an older brother and sister!”

Suddenly, the TimeWeb alarm went off. Tyler’s voice came over the loud-speaker. “Attention! Possible Viran activity! Ancient Greece. 454 BC. We need to check it out!”

Chapter 3

Even though the islanders had not come, the meeting went ahead anyway. The citizens gathered at the foot of a steep hill called the Acropolis. At the top stood the ruins of a beautiful temple.

Neena and Wilf easily found their way to the meeting. They followed the sound of cheering. The people were chanting the name 'Pericles' over and over again.

As they slipped in at the back of the crowd, Wilf received a download.

DOWNLOAD FROM TYLER

It's a General Assembly – like a big meeting. All the citizens will be asked to decide something.

Pericles stood up. He held up a wooden chest. Slowly he tipped it up. Thousands of silver coins cascaded to the ground.

"This money is payment from the islanders," began Pericles. "They pay a tax towards our navy, so that we can protect them from invaders. But they are outraged that we should want to use some of their money to rebuild our broken city."

Someone called out, "Why are the islanders not here to argue the case?" A murmur of agreement spread through the crowd.

Pericles raised a hand to silence them. "They are not coming!"

Once again the crowd murmured. Another councillor, called Hermippus, stood up. "But Pericles, the money the islanders give us is to pay for our navy so that we can protect them. That is all."

Pericles sighed. "But we do protect them! Our navy is strong. This money is left over. Surely it is ours to spend as we please?"

"But you want to use the money to improve Athens," argued Hermippus. "To pay for the city walls and to build a new temple on the Acropolis. How does that benefit the islanders?"

Pericles was angry. " 'To pay for the city walls'? Exactly! Our navy can't protect us if invaders come across the land. Surely their money can now be used to help us, so that we will be able to help them?"

The citizens began to cheer. “Build! Build!” they chanted.

An old councillor stood up. “We do not need a vote to decide. We’ll use the money to rebuild. It is the will of the people!”

Somewhere in the crowd, the old potter watched as Pericles knelt and began to put the silver coins back into the chest. The words, ‘The will of the people’ seemed to twist his mind into angry spasms. His head began to fill with the blackest of thoughts … of schemes and plots … of how to deny Athens this so-called ‘will of the people’ …

Chapter 4

From the shade of an olive tree, Wilf and Neena watched as the meeting broke up. Not far from where they sat, Pericles walked past. He was talking to a man who was carrying the chest of coins.

"Now the money belongs to Athens, the building of the great temple on the Acropolis can continue," Pericles said. He looked hard at the man. "I am trusting you with the people's money, Tektos.

Hermippus and some of the other councillors would love us to fail."

"I will use the money wisely, Pericles," Tektos smiled. "It will pay for more marble, stone masons, some slaves ... The money will be taken up to the building site at once."

Wilf spoke urgently into his Link. "What do you know about a leader called Pericles, Tyler? Oh, and see what you can find out about a 'great temple'."

"Will do!" came back the crackly sound of Tyler's voice. "But meanwhile, why not check out this 'great temple' yourselves?"

Chapter 5

Wilf and Neena climbed up the Acropolis. On the side of the hill, a group of slaves, some of them children, were digging a well. Wilf had an idea. "We are looking for work," he said. "Is there any? We are strong and willing to work hard."

The overseer in charge scratched his beard. "You'll have to speak to Tektos, the master-builder," he said gruffly. "He's in one of the huts at the great temple building site at the top. I'll take you up there."

In a hut at the top of the hill, Tektos was talking to the old potter, whose name was Bedros. He took some coins from the chest, to pay Bedros for some work he had done.

"And we'll need you to do some more as soon as possible," said Tektos as he bent down to lock the chest.

Bedros's mind filled with darkness. Without thinking, he picked up a heavy mallet and stepped silently towards the crouching figure of Tektos. His hands tensed. One more step and ...!

Suddenly, there was a bang on the door of the hut. "Who is it?" called Tektos.

At the door was the overseer. As if in a daze, Bedros pushed past him into the bright sunshine.

Tektos shuddered. "It's suddenly cold … gloomy," he muttered. He shook his head and looked at the overseer. "What?"

"Two strong-looking children asking for work," the overseer said. "Can we afford to take on more labour?"

Tektos glanced at the chest. "We can afford as many workers as you can get."

Chapter 6

Work on the temple was hard. It began at daybreak. Neena and Wilf had to help pull heavy blocks of marble up the slope on sledges. It was backbreaking work and the overseer would shout at them if they paused to rest. "Another of your great ideas, Wilf!" groaned Neena.

Work stopped as the last light of the day faded beyond the horizon. The slaves ate quickly with Tektos and the overseers.

Everyone slept soundly on the ground under the stars. The night throbbed to the sound of countless chirruping insects. No one stirred.

Bedros sat in his workshop staring into the flame of an oil lamp. Inwardly he cursed the Greeks – so orderly and rational. The will of the people! Democracy! Bedros's mind worked feverishly. How could he bring chaos to Athens? Perhaps by getting rid of Pericles? But how? If only he could get the people to lose confidence in Pericles like the islanders had. Suddenly he stood up. The islander's money! That was the key. That was the way to bring about chaos and downfall.

Silently, he slipped into the night.

A golden sun rose to reveal a scene of panic. A terrible cry had woken Wilf and Neena. It was Tektos. He was standing by his hut. The wooden door had been forced open. As people ran to him, Tektos sank to the ground and wept.

"The money …" he gasped. "The chest … The islander's money … Pericles trusted me with it. The building fund … It's gone. It's been stolen. All gone."

Chapter 7

The next day, Tektos stood in front of the citizens as they gathered for an urgent meeting. Athenian soldiers stood guard on either side of him.

Hermippus raised his arms to speak. "Citizens! This is an exceptional crime against Athens, and against the people of Athens. Tektos was entrusted with the money that has been stolen. I accuse Tektos of this terrible deed."

Pericles stood up. "This is an outrage! Where is your proof that he is guilty?"

Hermippus shook his head. "He may not be guilty of *theft*. But guilty he is!"

"What is your point?" asked Pericles.

"The money was in his care," snarled Hermippus. "He has betrayed our trust in him. And what do we tell the islanders? Do we tell them that their money is lost? That it has been wasted by stupidity?"

As the debate continued, Wilf whispered to Neena. "Tektos was asleep at the site. He'd locked the money away. It seems really unfair that he should get the blame."

A download came in from Tyler:

DOWNLOAD FROM TYLER

If the rebuilding is stopped, it will put Pericles in a difficult position. It was his idea. The people might turn against him.

Hermippus now had the people on his side. Many were cheering him on. “And who will have to pay for Pericles and Tektos’s mistake?” he asked. “You will. The people. Your taxes will have to make up the loss.”

Finally, an old councillor came foward. "Citizens. Since it affects us all, we must all decide. Such an unusual situation needs an unusual solution. I propose that, in seven days' time, we hold a *special* vote. If the councillors agree we will ask Bedros, the potter, to make the voting jars. If Tektos is found guilty of bringing shame upon us he will be banished. In the meantime, our soldiers will search every house in the city for the missing money. If the money is found, then the charges against Tektos will be dropped."

Chapter 8

Bedros sat deep in thought. So far, his plan had worked well. His eyes wandered over the many shelves of pots. He was not worried if the soldiers searched his workshop. He had hidden the money well, and burnt the wooden chest in his kiln. Then, when the time was right, he would smuggle the money past the guards on the city gates.

But he still had work to do. He had been asked to make the voting jars, but somehow he needed to make sure that the votes that were dropped into them would ensure Tektos was guilty. That way, Pericles was certain to fall from power. But how could he be sure that the vote went against Tektos?

His eyes settled upon the crates of shattered pottery that had been broken at the harbour. Suddenly, he had it! His hand reached for a needle-sharp blade. He knew exactly what he was going to do.

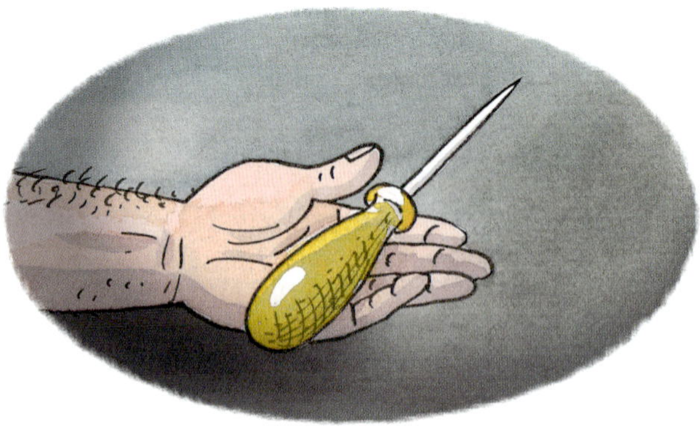

Chapter 9

Despite the week-long search, the money was not found. And so the day of the vote finally came. As the people gathered, Bedros arrived with three large clay jars.

"They must be really heavy," said Wilf. "Look!"

With great difficulty, Bedros struggled to unload the jars from his cart.

"Each of you knows what you have to do," shouted the old councillor. "Find yourself a piece of broken pottery. Then scratch the word 'guilty' on it – or 'not guilty' if you think Tektos should go free. Cast your vote into one of the jars. You have until sunset."

Finally, dusk fell on Athens. The citizens had cast their votes and the time had come to count them.

Everyone gathered to hear the result of the vote. Flaming torches lit the faces of the councillors as they called for quiet. "We have the result! The citizens of Athens find Tektos ... guilty! He must be banished. He has brought shame upon us all. He will be sent from the city at dawn. It is the will of the people."

That night, everyone in Athens slept well. Justice had been done. Only Tektos remained awake in his prison cell, hoping for a miracle.

Chapter 10

Neena woke from a restless sleep. She could hear strange noises in the still night air. She nudged Wilf awake, and they crept down the hill towards the sound. A shadowy figure was tipping something down the well. Wilf took out his Zaptrap, but Neena held his arm. "Wait!" she hissed.

"We have to be sure! He may not be a Viran!"

Eventually the figure finished his task and faded into the darkness.

"Quickly! Get a torch, Wilf," urged Neena. "We need to see what was thrown down there."

With Wilf holding a flaming torch above the well, Neena climbed down. At the bottom she stood shin-deep in water. "What can you see?" Wilf hissed.

"Loads of broken pottery. It looks like they are from the vote." Neena studied piece after piece. But something was not right. Some of the pieces said 'not guilty'. But most of them had the chilling word 'guilty' scratched on them.

"Quick, Wilf, pull me up," said Neena. "I think I've worked it out!"

Kneeling in the dirt, Neena laid out some bits of pottery she had brought up from the well. "Look at the design on each piece," she said.

Wilf looked closely. Broken images of Greek gods, mythical heroes and strange beasts flickered by the light of his torch.

"I don't see ..." he mumbled.

"It looks like all these pieces come from pots made by the same potter. There are hundreds more like that down in the well. And I bet every single one of those has the word 'guilty' scraped on them," Neena explained.

Wilf fitted some pieces together. "Look! These bits even come from the very same pot," he said. "How likely is it that everyone in Athens all used pieces of pot that came from the same potter?"

"And look at the word 'guilty'," added Neena. "It's the same handwriting on all of them! Someone has added all these pieces, to make sure Tektos was found guilty!"

"So the vote was rigged!" said Wilf. "I bet it was that potter who was asked to make the voting jars. Remember when he brought the jars? He struggled to move them. I bet all these pieces were already in the jars."

"And I bet if we find him, we'll find the stolen money," added Neena. She opened her Link. "Tyler, quickly! Can you find any records of potters who lived in Athens?"

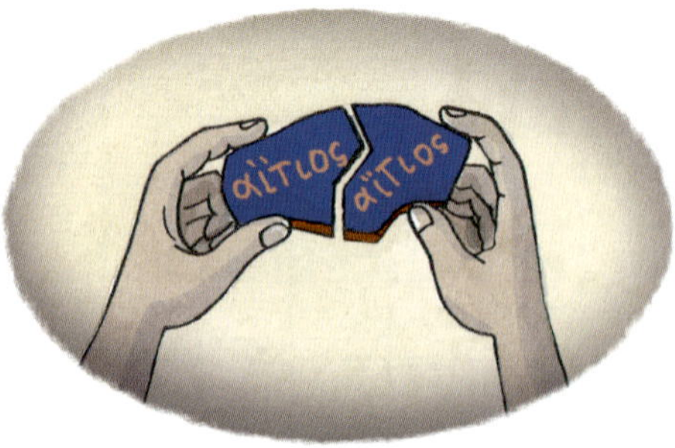

Chapter 11

Bedros worked quickly, loading his pots on to a cart. His plan was working. With Tektos banished and the money missing, the people would surely turn against Pericles. Athens would be in chaos!

All he had to do now was to smuggle the money out of Athens. He smiled as he lifted another pot on to the wagon. The money's hiding place was so cunning that getting past the guards on the city gates would be easy.

Suddenly, Bedros sniffed the air, sensing someone was near. From the dark streets two children appeared. Neena and Wilf stopped in their tracks.

They hadn't expected to come across the potter so easily.

Something about the two children made Bedros's skin prickle uncomfortably. His mind filled with the blackest of thoughts. It took all his will to keep calm. "Can I help you?" he mumbled, reluctantly.

"Er ..." muttered Wilf. He stepped closer. "We've been sent by the councillors. They need to see you."

"Not possible. I am busy. I am going to the market in Thebes," Bedros lied. "It's a long journey. I should be gone already."

Neena could see a problem. If the potter was a Viran, they couldn't zap him until they had found the money, otherwise it might be lost forever. She wondered if it might be hidden in the pots. “Do you need help loading the cart?” she asked.

“Please yourself,” muttered Bedros.

Neena picked up a large pot. It was heavy, but empty. Odd. Neena began to worry. Maybe this potter wasn’t the Viran?

“Which of the councillors sent you?” Bedros asked casually.

Neena took a chance. “Mortlock!”

Startled by the name, Bedros dropped the pot he was holding. It shattered on the stony ground. Stuck to the inside of the pot, in a thin layer of raw clay, were dozens of silver coins. The *stolen* coins!

The Viran in Bedros rose to the surface. His face twisted like a fanged snake. In seconds the golden light of the dawn sun had vanished in a choking black mist.

The Viran lurched towards them. But Wilf was too quick. His Zaptrap zoomed like an angry wasp through the darkness. In a flash of light and crackling sparks, the Viran was blasted. The Zaptrap snapped shut. "Job done!" smiled Wilf, as he picked it up.

Neena smashed open more pots. Each one was lined with coins. "It's a good job the Viran dropped that pot, or we might never have found the money."

"I guess you could say it was pot luck!" smirked Wilf.

Glossary

banished *(page 33)* Sent away from home in disgrace. *He must be banished.*

citizens *(page 12)* The citizens of Athens were the people who were allowed to vote about how Athens was governed. They were all free men (not slaves, and not women). *The citizens gathered at the foot of a steep hill called the Acropolis.*

councillors *(page 7)* Members of a council whose job is to plan and discuss how to run a city or town. *"The Athenian councillors!"*

debated *(page 8)* A debate is a formal discussion in which people decide what to do by comparing alternative options. *"Our idea needs to be debated by the people …"*

overseer *(page 21)* The person in charge of the work. *At the door was the overseer.*

quayside *(page 3)* The side of a harbour or pier where ships are tied up for loading and unloading. *Beside him, on the busy quayside, were crates of his pots, jugs and bowls.*

rational *(page 23)* If a person is rational, they always want to have a reason for everything they do. *Inwardly he cursed the Greeks – so orderly and rational.*

Thesaurus: Another word for …

rational *(page 23)* reasonable, sensible, cautious.

Tyler's Mission Report

Location:	Date:
Athens, Greece.	454 BC
Mission Status:	**Viran Status:**
Successful.	1 zaptrapped.

Notes: Voting with bits of pot!

Democracy seems like a good idea to me. It means that power is given to those with the best ideas, rather than the sharpest swords. What's more, the ideas have to be successful or the people will get rid of them and try someone else's ideas instead.

Another thing. Giving people a say makes them feel part of a place. It makes them feel they belong. That said, not all the people had the right to vote in Ancient Athens. Women, non-Athenians and slaves made up a large part of the population, but had no say in how it was run. Believe me, as someone who lived on the streets, it's a terrible thing to feel that you have no say, and that you don't really belong.

Sign off: ....Tyler..............

History: downloaded!

Ancient Athens

The Parthenon

On one of their highest hills, the Athenians built a magnificent temple in honour of the goddess Athena.

Being so high meant it could be seen for miles around. What do you suppose it said about Athens, to a passing stranger from another city-state? What did it symbolize?

Perhaps it symbolized the growing confidence that Athens was doing well. Perhaps the stranger might think about his own city-state and wish it were more like Athens. After all, everyone in Ancient Greece spoke the same language and believed in the same gods. So what was it about Athens that was so special?

Pericles

Might it be the strong army or even stronger navy? So strong in fact, that Athens now offered protection to other city-states from any threat of invasion. Perhaps it was that the Athenians had found silver, lots of it, on their land. Or trade perhaps? They were great tradespeople.

Maybe it was because they attracted the great thinkers of the time – the philosophers, the artists, the playwrights.

Or could it be that they had democracy? Could it be that asking the people what they thought, meant that the city was run according to the best and most popular ideas?

For more information, see the Time Chronicles website:
www.oxfordprimary.co.uk/timechronicles

A voice from history

If I told you the columns on this temple all lean slightly inward, would you believe me? You'd probably think I was mad. Everyone knows you have to build in straight lines, right?

If you had to vote for someone to build the temple, would I get the job? Would you vote for me? I thought not.

Yet the secret to building is to make things look straight. But this don't always mean they actually are. The eye plays tricks, you see. We builders understand this.

Do the people know best? I'm not sure they do. I ain't no public speaker, I'm a builder. You'd probably vote for the fella who spoke best, not for me. But you'd be wrong. Just because lots of people vote for it, it don't always mean it's right.